TOWER

Air Fryer

Cookbook

Delicious Recipes for Your Tower T17021

Family Size Air Fryer

Molly Sartain

CONTENTS

Introduction..**6**

How Does an Air Fryer Work?...6

10 Reasons to Buy an Air Fryer..6

HOW TO USE AN AIR FRYER...8

Five Tips for Using an Air Fryer..9

Breakfast & Brunch Recipes...**10**

Peppers and Lettuce Salad...10

Italian Sausage Patties..11

Beans Oatmeal..12

Morning Mushroom Frittata...13

Omelette Frittata..14

Potato Rosti...15

Bread Cups Omelette...16

Hash Brown...17

Gourmet Cheesy Bread...18

Crispy Potato Rosti..19

Eggs Salad..20

Lunch & Dinner Recipes..**21**

Cheese Quiche..21

Baby Back Ribs..22

Monkey Salad...23

Rice Bowl..24

Herbed Butter Beef Loin...25

Parmesan Chicken..26

Bacon & Chicken Patties...27

Vegetable Salad..28

Rosemary Salmon..29

Cauliflower Rice Chicken Curry..30

Duck Fat Ribeye...31

Desserts Recipes..**32**

Easy 'n Delicious Brownies..32

Ninja Pop-tarts...33

Glazed Donuts..34

Cherry-choco Bars...35

Orange Muffins...36

Layered Cake..37

Hazelnut Brownie Cups..38

Swirled German Cake..39

Lemon Berry Jam...40

Red Velvet Cupcakes...41

Berry Pie...42

Beef, pork & Lamb Recipes..**43**

Roasted Ribeye Steak with Rum..43

Shepherd's Pie Made of Ground Lamb...44

Grilled Tri Tip Over Beet Salad...46

Leftover Beef and Kale Omelet...47

Pork with Balsamic-raspberry Jam..48

Peppermint Lamb...49

Beef Bulgogi..50

Family Pork Loin Roast..51

Bbq Skirt Steak...52

Spicy Lamb Kebabs..53

Hot Paprika Beef..54

Poultry Recipes...**55**

Bbq Pineapple 'n Teriyaki Glazed Chicken..55

Turkey Loaf...56

Tangy Chicken with Parsley and Lime..57

Sausage, Ham and Hash Brown Bake..58

Quick 'n Easy Garlic Herb Wings..59

Lebanese Style Grilled Chicken..60

Chicken Egg Rolls with Hot Dipping Sauce...61

Fried Chicken Legs...62

Crispy Chicken Thighs...63

Lemon-oregano Chicken Bbq..64

Easy Turkey Breasts with Basil..65

Lime and Mustard Marinated Chicken..66

Fish & Seafood Recipes..**67**

Wrapped Scallops...67

Juicy Salmon and Asparagus Parcels..68

Tuna Stuffed Avocado...69

Bacon Wrapped Scallops...70

Spicy Prawns...71

Fennel Salad Topped with Roast Salmon..72

Creamed Trout Salad...73

Butter Paprika Swordfish..74

Glazed Halibut Steak...75

Pollock with Kalamata Olives and Capers..76

Shrimp Magic...77

Snacks & Appetizers Recipes..**78**

Sweet Corn and Bell Pepper Sandwich with Barbecue Sauce................................78

Sweet and Spicy Carrot Sticks..79

Juicy Meatballs...80

Bruschetta with Fresh Tomato and Basil...81

Spicy Broccoli Poppers..82

Crunchy Bacon Bites..83

Onion Rings...84

Baked Tortillas..85

Roasted Peppers..86

Garlic Potatoes..87

Decadent Brie and Pork Meatballs...88

Vegan & Vegetarian Recipes..**89**

    Roasted Pepper Salad with Goat Cheese.. 89

    Hasselback Potatoes.. 90

    Tangy Asparagus and Broccoli..91

    Poblano & Tomato Stuffed Squash... 92

    Baked Spicy Tortilla Chips... 93

    Zoodles with Cheese..94

    Herby Veggie Cornish Pasties...95

    Tofu In Sweet & Spicy Sauce..96

    Fried Broccoli Recipe from India.. 97

    Crisped Tofu with Paprika.. 98

    Veggies Stuffed Eggplants.. 99

Vegetable & Side Dishes...**100**

    Thyme & Garlic Sweet Potato Wedges.. 100

    Mint Fennel and Berry Mix... 101

    Turmeric Cauliflower Rice.. 102

    Balsamic and Garlic Cabbage Mix..102

    Simple Tomatoes and Bell Pepper Sauce Recipe.. 103

    Homemade Croquettes..104

    Kabocha Fries...104

    Cilantro Broccoli Mix... 105

    Cauliflower Falafel... 106

    Cumin Brussels Sprouts..107

    Turkey Garlic Potatoes... 108

INTRODUCTION

How Does an Air Fryer Work?

The first think you're probably wondering is how an Air Fryer works. How is it any different than a regular deep fryer or an oven? Most importantly, Air Fryers are different from regular deep fryers because they don't actually fry food, meaning you don't actually submerge your food in hot oil to cook it.

The actual mechanism of Air Fryers is most akin to that of a convection oven. Basically, your food is placed in a perforated metal basket. At the top is a heating unit with a high powered fan that blows the hot air all around the food, creating a convection effect that nicely and evenly browns the outside of the food. and unlike a convection oven, Air Fryers are compact, allowing for faster and more efficient preheating and cooking times.

10 Reasons to Buy an Air Fryer

1) It makes delicious food !

When you bake food in regular ovens (especially not convention ovens), you are often left with uneven results, with some parts burnt and other parts undercooked. The mechanism of Air Fryers described above allows hot air to circulate all around the food, maximizing surface area-to-heat ratio and allowing for perfectly even crispiness and crunchiness. While an Air Fryer won't taste exactly like if you used a traditional deep fryer, we really love the end result of each recipe we've tried so far.

2) It is a healthier option

Love the taste of fried food but not the way it makes you feel afterwards (for instance Zoe tends to get heartburn with fried food)? Are you disappointed with the end result when you try the oven-roasted version of the same recipe? If yes to these questions, then an Air Fryer might be the solution!

You can usually get away with using little-to-no oil when cooking with an Air Fryer, which can cut calories. Furthermore, one study (Sansano et at., 2015) showed that compared to traditional frying methods, using an air fryer reduces acrylamide (a compound associated with certain types of cancer) by up to 90%.

3) It is time and energy efficient

With their compact size and efficient circulation of hot air, Air Fryers out-compete your oven. with most recipes only needing 8-20 minutes of cooking, Air Fryers reduce cooking time by up to 25% (they also only need a fraction of the time to preheat, unlike your oven), saving you both time and energy.

4) There's an air fryer for every price range

With prices as low as $40, buying an Air Fryer doesn't have to break your wallet. We are obviously more than happy with our investment in an Air Fryer. and don't worry, even the lower-priced ones still produce great results! Keep reading this Ultimate Air Fryer Guide to see the specific products we recommend.

5) They are easy to clean

With removable parts, nonstick materials, and most being dishwasher-safe, cleaning your air fryer is no hassle at all! and compared to the grease that coats your kitchen walls after deep frying foods, an Air Fryer produces no mess.

6) They are versatile and can make all kinds of recipes

See below for a sample of all of the different types of food you can make using an Air Fryer. from meat to vegetables to even pizza, we've been able to incorporate air frying into a ton of our meal preparations.

7) Many have different modes, allowing different types of cooking

Not only used for frying foods, an Air Fryer can also be used for reheating leftovers, thawing frozen food, and much, much more. Ours lets you change the settings to "air fry", "roast", "dehydrate", and "reheat". It's up to you to experiment!

8) They come in all different shapes and sizes

It's true that they take up some counter space. But there's an Air Fryer of every size to fit your needs. If you mostly cook for one or two people, you can get away with 2 to 3 quart sized Air Fryers. If you usually cook for a family of 3-5, consider 5 to 6 quart ones. But generally, air fryers between 3 to 5 quarts are versatile enough for most types and quantities of cooking.

9) They make for a great gift

What a perfect gift for the budding home chef?! I got ours for Zoe for Christmas. But whether its for a birthday, wedding registry, or any other special occasion, an Air Fryer makes for an ideal long-lasting and useful present.

10) Thcy lct you join the Air Fryer community

With niche Air Fryer blogs to Air Fryer recipe books, buying one of these lets you drastically expand your culinary repertoire and connect with a whole new community of home chefs.

HOW TO USE AN AIR FRYER

The Air Fryer's Versatility

Get ready to challenge everything you know about frying foods. Air fryers can fry your favorite foods to crispy, golden brown perfection (yes, French fries and potato chips!) using little or no oil. Not only can you make traditionally fried foods like potato chips and French fries, but it's also great for vegetables, proteins like chicken wings and drummettes, and appetizers like coquettes and feta triangles. Even desserts like brownies and blondies are perfectly baked in an air fryer.

Why It Works

Put in other terms, an air fryer is much like a convection oven but in a different outfit, cooking food at very high temperatures while simultaneously circulating dry air around the food, cooking food faster all the while making it crisp without needing to add extra fat.

What to Look for in an Air Fryer

There are a lot of different sizes and types of air fryers available now. If you're cooking for a crowd, try an the Philips XXL Air Fryer which can cook an entire chicken or six portions of fries.

If you have limited counter space, try the Philips Avance Air Fryer which uses patented technology to circulate hot air, yielding crunchy, satisfying results. and this next-generation air fryer boasts a more compact size (same capacity!) and TurboStar technology, which ensures food cooks evenly (no more worrying about pile-ups). Now you can enjoy all the fried foods you love—without the guilt.

To up an air fryer's versatility even more, You can also buy a variety of different attachments, such as a rack, grill pan, muffin pans and mesh baskets) to for entertaining. Check out our Air Fryer seasonings that we developed in-house, ranging from Buttermilk Black Pepper Seasoning for air-frying chicken to Garlic Sichuan Seasoning perfect for Chinese cooking.

Read on for a video on the air fryer in action, how-to tips and our favorite recipes, including those fries, air-fried tonkotsu, chicken wings and more.

Five Tips for Using an Air Fryer

1. Shake it.

Be sure to open the air fryer and shake foods around as they "fry" in the machine's basket—smaller foods like French fries and chips can compress. For best results, rotate them every 5-10 minutes.

2. Don't overcrowd.

Give foods plenty of space so that the air can circulate effectively; that's what gives you crispy results. Our test kitchen cooks swear by the air fryer for snacks and small batches.

3. Give foods a spray.

Lightly spray foods with cooking spray or add just a bit of oil to ensure they don't stick to the basket.

4. Keep it dry.

Pat foods dry before cooking (if they are marinated, for example) to avoid splattering and excess smoke. Similarly, when cooking high-fat foods like chicken wings, make sure to empty the fat from the bottom machine periodically.

5. Master other cooking methods.

The air fryer isn't just for frying; it's great for other healthy cooking methods like baking, roasting and grilling, too. Our test kitchen also loves to use the machine for cooking salmon!

BREAKFAST & BRUNCH RECIPES

Peppers and Lettuce Salad

Servings: 4
Cooking Time: 10 Mins.

Ingredients:
- 1 tbsp. lime juice
- 4 red bell peppers
- 1 lettuce head, torn
- Salt and black pepper to taste
- 3 tbsps. heavy cream
- 2 tbsps. olive oil
- 2 ozs. rocket leaves

Directions:
1. Place the bell peppers in your air fryer's basket and cook at 400 degrees F for 10 minutes.
2. Remove the peppers, peel, cut them into strips, and put them in a bowl.
3. Add all remaining ingredients, toss, and serve.

Italian Sausage Patties

Servings: 4
Cooking Time: 20 Mins.

Ingredients:
- ¼ cup breadcrumbs
- 1 tsp dried parsley
- 1 tsp red pepper flakes
- ½ tsp salt
- ¼ tsp black pepper
- ¼ tsp garlic powder
- 1 egg, beaten

Directions:
1. Preheat air fryer to 350 F. Combine all the ingredients in a large bowl. Make patties out of the mixture and arrange them on a greased baking sheet. Cook in the air fryer for 15 minutes, flipping once.

Beans Oatmeal

Servings: 2
Cooking Time: 15 Mins.

Ingredients:
- 1 cup steel cut oats
- 2 tbsps. canned kidney beans, drained
- 2 red bell peppers, chopped
- 4 tbsps. heavy cream
- Salt and black pepper to taste
- ¼ tsp. cumin, ground

Directions:
1. Heat up your air fryer at 360 degrees F and add all ingredients; stir.
2. Cover and cook for 15 minutes.
3. Divide into bowls, serve, and enjoy!

Morning Mushroom Frittata

Servings: 4
Cooking Time: 20 Mins.

Ingredients:
- ½ cup heavy cream
- Salt and black pepper to taste
- 2 cups mushrooms, sliced
- 1 red onion, chopped
- ½ cup diced tomato
- 1 cup shredded mozzarella cheese
- Parsley for garnishing

Directions:
1. Preheat the Air Fryer to 350 F. Grease a baking dish with cooking spray and set aside.
2. In a bowl, whisk the eggs, add in heavy cream, mushrooms, onion, tomatoes, mozzarella cheese, salt, and pepper. Mix to combine. Pour the mixture in the baking dish and cook in the air fryer for 15 minutes, or until the eggs are set. Sprinkle with parsley and cut into wedges to serve.

Omelette Frittata

Servings: 2
Cooking Time: 6 Mins.

Ingredients:
- 3 eggs, lightly beaten
- 2 tbsp cheddar cheese, shredded
- 2 tbsp heavy cream
- 2 mushrooms, sliced
- 1/4 small onion, chopped
- 1/4 bell pepper, diced
- Pepper
- Salt

Directions:
1. In a bowl, whisk eggs with cream, vegetables, pepper, and salt.
2. Preheat the air fryer to 400 F.
3. Pour egg mixture into the air fryer pan. Place pan in air fryer basket and cook for 5 minutes.
4. Add shredded cheese on top of the frittata and cook for 1 minute more.
5. Serve and enjoy.

Potato Rosti

Servings: 2
Cooking Time: 15 Mins.

Ingredients:
- 1 tsp. olive oil
- ½ lb. russet potatoes, peeled and roughly grated
- 1 tbsp. fresh chives, finely chopped
- Salt and ground black pepper, as required
- 2 tbsps. sour cream
- 3½ ozs. smoked salmon, cut into slices

Directions:
1. Set the temperature of Air Fryer to 355 degrees F. Grease a pizza pan with the olive oil.
2. In a large bowl, mix together the potatoes, chives, salt, and black pepper.
3. Place the potato mixture into the prepared pizza pan.
4. Arrange the pan in an Air Fryer basket.
5. Air Fry for about 15 minutes or until the top becomes golden brown.
6. Cut the potato rosti into wedges.
7. Top with the sour cream and smoked salmon slices and serve immediately.

Bread Cups Omelette

Servings: 4
Cooking Time: 25 Mins.

Ingredients:
- 5 eggs, beaten
- A pinch of salt
- ½ tsp thyme, dried
- 3 strips precooked bacon, chopped
- 2 tbsp heavy cream
- 4 Gouda cheese mini wedges, thin slices

Directions:
1. Preheat your air fryer 330 F. Cut the tops off the rolls and remove the inside with your fingers. Line the rolls with a slice of cheese and press down, so the cheese conforms to the inside of the roll. In a bowl, mix eggs with heavy cream, bacon, thyme, salt and pepper.
2. Stuff the rolls with the egg mixture. Lay the rolls in your air fryer's cooking basket and bake for 8 to 12 minutes or until the eggs become puffy and the roll shows a golden brown texture.

Hash Brown

Servings: 2
Cooking Time: 20 Mins.

Ingredients:
- 12 oz grated fresh cauliflower (about ½ a medium-sized head)
- 4 slices bacon, chopped
- 3 oz onion, chopped
- 1 tbsp butter, softened

Directions:
1. In a skillet, sauté the bacon and onion until brown.
2. Add in the cauliflower and stir until tender and browned.
3. Add the butter steadily as it cooks.
4. Season to taste with salt and pepper.
5. Enjoy!

Gourmet Cheesy Bread

Servings: 2
Cooking Time: 15 Mins.

Ingredients:

- 3 bread slices
- 2 tbsps. cheddar cheese
- 2 eggs, whites and yolks, separated
- 1 tbsp. chives
- 1 tbsp. olives
- 1 tbsp. mustard
- 1 tbsp. paprika

Directions:

1. Preheat the Air fryer to 355 F and place the bread slices in a fryer basket.
2. Cook for about 5 minutes until toasted and dish out.
3. Whisk together egg whites in a bowl until soft peaks form.
4. Mix together cheese, egg yolks, mustard and paprika in another bowl until well combined.
5. Fold in egg whites gently and spread the mustard mixture over toasted bread slices.
6. Place in the Air fryer and cook for about 10 minutes.
7. Remove from the Air fryer and serve warm.

Crispy Potato Rosti

Servings: 2

Cooking Time: 15 Mins.

Ingredients:
- ½ lb. russet potatoes, peeled and grated roughly
- 1 tbsp. chives, chopped finely
- 2 tbsps. shallots, minced
- 1/8 cup cheddar cheese
- 3.5 ozs. smoked salmon, cut into slices
- 2 tbsps. sour cream
- 1 tbsp. olive oil
- Salt and black pepper, to taste

Directions:
1. Preheat the Air fryer to 365 F and grease a pizza pan with the olive oil.
2. Mix together potatoes, shallots, chives, cheese, salt and black pepper in a large bowl until well combined.
3. Transfer the potato mixture into the prepared pizza pan and place in the Air fryer basket.
4. Cook for about 15 minutes and dish out in a platter.
5. Cut the potato rosti into wedges and top with smoked salmon slices and sour cream to serve.

Eggs Salad

Servings: 4
Cooking Time: 10 Mins.

Ingredients:
- 1 tbsp. lime juice
- 4 eggs, hard boiled, peeled and sliced
- 2 cups baby spinach
- Salt and black pepper to the taste
- 3 tbsps. heavy cream
- 2 tbsps. olive oil

Directions:
1. In your Air Fryer, mix the spinach with cream, eggs, salt and pepper, cover and cook at 360 degrees F for 6 minutes. Transfer this to a bowl, add the lime juice and oil, toss and serve for breakfast.

LUNCH & DINNER RECIPES

Cheese Quiche

Servings: 5
Cooking Time: 19 Mins.

Ingredients:
- ½ cup almond flour
- 1 tbsp. Psyllium husk
- ½ tsp. flax meal
- ¼ tsp. baking powder
- 2 eggs, beaten
- 7 oz Feta cheese, crumbled
- ¼ cup scallions, diced
- ½ tsp. ground black pepper
- ¼ tsp. ground cardamom
- 1 oz Parmesan, grated
- 1 tsp. coconut oil, melted
- 3 tbsps. almond butter

Directions:
1. Make the quiche crust: mix up almond flour, Psyllium husk, flax meal, baking powder, and almond butter in the bowl. Stir the mixture until homogenous and knead the non-sticky dough. Then pour melted coconut oil in the skillet and bring it to boil. Add scallions and cook it for 3 minutes or until it is light brown. Then transfer the cooked onion in the mixing bowl. Add Parmesan, ground cardamom, and ground black pepper. After this, add Feta cheese and eggs. Stir the mass until homogenous. Cut the dough into 5 pieces. Place the dough in the quiche molds and flatten it in the shape of the pie crust with the help of the fingertips. Then fill every quiche crust with a Feta mixture. Preheat the air fryer to 365F. Put the molds with quiche in the air fryer basket and cook them for 15 minutes.

Baby Back Ribs

Servings: 2
Cooking Time: 45 Mins.

Ingredients:
- 2 tsp. red pepper flakes
- ¾ ground ginger
- 3 cloves minced garlic
- Salt and pepper
- 2 baby back ribs

Directions:
1. Pre-heat your fryer at 350°F.
2. Combine the red pepper flakes, ginger, garlic, salt and pepper in a bowl, making sure to mix well. Massage the mixture into the baby back ribs.
3. Cook the ribs in the fryer for thirty minutes.
4. Take care when taking the rubs out of the fryer. Place them on a serving dish and enjoy with a low-carb barbecue sauce of your choosing.

Monkey Salad

Servings: 1
Cooking Time: 10 Mins.

Ingredients:
- 2 tbsp butter
- 1 cup unsweetened coconut flakes
- 1 cup raw, unsalted cashews
- 1 cup raw, unsalted s
- 1 cup 90% dark chocolate shavings

Directions:
1. In a skillet, melt the butter on a medium heat.
2. Add the coconut flakes and sauté until lightly browned for 4 minutes.
3. Add the cashews and s and sauté for 3 minutes. Remove from the heat and sprinkle with dark chocolate shavings.
4. Serve!

Rice Bowl

Servings: 4
Cooking Time: 55 Mins.

Ingredients:
- ¼ cup cucumber, sliced
- 1 tsp. salt
- 1 tbsp. sugar
- 7 tbsp. Japanese rice vinegar
- 3 medium-sized eggplants, sliced
- 3 tbsp. sweet white miso paste
- 1 tbsp. mirin rice wine
- 4 cups sushi rice, cooked
- 4 spring onions
- 1 tbsp. sesame seeds, toasted

Directions:
1. Coat the cucumber slices with the rice wine vinegar, salt, and sugar.
2. Place a dish on top of the bowl to weight it down completely.
3. Pre-heat the Air Fryer at 400°F.
4. In a bowl, mix together the eggplants, mirin rice wine, and miso paste. Allow to marinate for half an hour.
5. Cook the eggplant in the fryer for 10 minutes.
6. Place the eggplant slices in the Air Fryer and cook for 10 minutes.
7. Fill the bottom of a serving bowl with rice and top with the eggplants and pickled cucumbers. Add the spring onions and sesame seeds for garnish.

Herbed Butter Beef Loin

Servings: 4
Cooking Time: 25 Mins.

Ingredients:
- 1 tbsp. butter, melted
- ¼ dried thyme
- 1 tsp. garlic salt
- ¼ tsp. dried parsley
- 1 lb. beef loin

Directions:
1. In a bowl, combine the melted butter, thyme, garlic salt, and parsley.
2. Cut the beef loin into slices and generously apply the seasoned butter using a brush.
3. Pre-heat your fryer at 400°F and place a rack inside.
4. Cook the beef for fifteen minutes.
5. Take care when removing it and serve hot.

Parmesan Chicken

Servings: 4
Cooking Time: 30 Mins.

Ingredients:
- 1 tsp. olive oil
- 4 spring onions, chopped
- 2 chicken breasts, skinless, boneless and cubed
- Salt and black pepper to the taste
- 1 and ½ cups parmesan cheese, grated
- ½ cup keto tomato sauce

Directions:
1. Preheat your air fryer at 400 degrees F, add half of the oil and the spring onions and fry them for 8 minutes, shaking the fryer halfway. Add the rest of the ingredients, toss, cook at 370 degrees F for 22 minutes, shaking the fryer halfway as well. Divide between plates and serve for lunch.

Bacon & Chicken Patties

Servings: 2

Cooking Time: 15 Mins.

Ingredients:

- 1 ½ oz can chicken breast
- 4 slices bacon
- ¼ cup parmesan cheese
- 1 large egg
- 3 tbsp flour

Directions:

1. Cook the bacon until crispy.
2. Chop the chicken and bacon together in a food processor until fine.
3. Add in the parmesan, egg, flour and mix.
4. Make the patties by hand and fry on a medium heat in a pan with some oil.
5. Once browned, flip over, continue cooking, and lie them to drain.
6. Serve!

Vegetable Salad

Servings: 4
Cooking Time: 20 Mins.

Ingredients:
- 6 plum tomatoes, halved
- 2 large red onions, sliced
- 4 long red pepper, sliced
- 2 yellow pepper, sliced
- 6 cloves of garlic, crushed
- 1 tbsp. extra-virgin olive oil
- 1 tsp. paprika
- ½ lemon, juiced
- Salt and pepper to taste
- 1 tbsp. baby capers

Directions:
1. Pre-heat the Air Fryer at 420°F.
2. Put the tomatoes, onions, peppers, and garlic in a large bowl and cover with the extra virgin olive oil, paprika, and lemon juice. Sprinkle with salt and pepper as desired.
3. Line the inside of your fryer with aluminum foil. Place the vegetables inside and allow to cook for 10 minutes, ensuring the edges turn brown.
4. Serve in a salad bowl with the baby capers. Make sure all the ingredients are well combined.

Rosemary Salmon

Servings: 2
Cooking Time: 7 Mins.

Ingredients:
- 4 oz Feta cheese, sliced
- 1 lemon slice, chopped
- ½ tsp. dried rosemary
- 1 tsp. apple cider vinegar
- ½ tsp. ground paprika
- 1-pound salmon fillet
- 1 tsp. olive oil
- ½ tsp. salt
- Cooking spray

Directions:
1. Rub the salmon with dried rosemary and salt. Then sprinkle the fish with ground paprika and apple cider vinegar. Preheat the air fryer to 395F. Line the air fryer basket with baking paper and put the salmon fillet on it. Spray it with cooking spray and cook for 3 minutes. Then flip the salmon on another side and cook it for 4 minutes more. After this, cut the cooked salmon into 2 servings and put it on the serving plate. Top the fish with sliced feta and chopped lemon slice. Sprinkle the meal with the olive oil before serving.

Cauliflower Rice Chicken Curry

Servings: 4
Cooking Time: 40 Mins.

Ingredients:
- 2 lb chicken (4 breasts)
- 1 packet curry paste
- 3 tbsp ghee (can substitute with butter)
- ½ cup heavy cream
- 1 head cauliflower (around 1 kg/2.2 lb)

Directions:
1. Melt the ghee in a pot. Mix in the curry paste.
2. Add the water and simmer for 5 minutes.
3. Add the chicken, cover, and simmer on a medium heat for 20 minutes or until the chicken is cooked.
4. Shred the cauliflower florets in a food processor to resemble rice.
5. Once the chicken is cooked, uncover, and incorporate the cream.
6. Cook for 7 minutes and serve over the cauliflower.

Duck Fat Ribeye

Servings: 1

Cooking Time: 20 Mins.

Ingredients:
- One 16-oz ribeye steak (1 - 1 ¼ inch thick)
- 1 tbsp duck fat (or other high smoke point oil like peanut oil)
- ½ tbsp butter
- ½ tsp thyme, chopped
- Salt and pepper to taste

Directions:
1. Preheat a skillet in your fryer at 400°F/200°C.
2. Season the steaks with the oil, salt and pepper. Remove the skillet from the fryer once pre-heated.
3. Put the skillet on your stove top burner on a medium heat and drizzle in the oil.
4. Sear the steak for 1-4 minutes, depending on if you like it rare, medium or well done.
5. Turn over the steak and place in your fryer for 6 minutes.
6. Take out the steak from your fryer and place it back on the stove top on low heat.
7. Toss in the butter and thyme and cook for 3 minutes, basting as you go along.
8. Rest for 5 minutes and serve.

DESSERTS RECIPES

Easy 'n Delicious Brownies

Servings: 8
Cooking Time: 20 Mins.

Ingredients:
- 1/4 cup butter
- 1/2 cup white sugar
- 1 egg
- 1/2 tsp. vanilla extract
- 2 tbsps. and 2 tsps. unsweetened cocoa powder
- 1/4 cup all-purpose flour
- 1/8 tsp. salt
- 1/8 tsp. baking powder
- 1 tbsp. and 1-1/2 tsps. butter, softened
- 1 tbsp. and 1-1/2 tsps. unsweetened cocoa powder
- 1-1/2 tsps. honey
- 1/2 tsp. vanilla extract
- 1/2 cup confectioners' sugar

Directions:
1. Lightly grease baking pan of air fryer with cooking spray. Melt ¼ cup butter for 3 minutes. Stir in vanilla, eggs, and sugar. Mix well.
2. Stir in baking powder, salt, flour, and cocoa mix well. Evenly spread.
3. For 20 minutes, cook on 300oF.
4. In a small bowl, make the frosting by mixing well all Ingredients. Frost brownies while still warm.
5. Serve and enjoy.

Ninja Pop-tarts

Servings: 6
Cooking Time: 1 Hour

Ingredients:
- Pop-tarts:
- 1 cup coconut flour
- 1 cup almond flour
- ½ cup of ice-cold water
- Pop-tarts:
- ¼ tsp. salt
- 2 tbsps. swerve
- 2/3 cup very cold coconut oil
- ½ tsp. vanilla extract
- Lemon Glaze:
- 1¼ cups powdered swerve
- 2 tbsps. lemon juice
- zest of 1 lemon
- 1 tsp. coconut oil, melted
- ¼ tsp. vanilla extract

Directions:
1. Pop-tarts:
2. Preheat the Air fryer to 375 F and grease an Air fryer basket.
3. Mix all the flours, swerve, and salt in a bowl and stir in the coconut oil.
4. Mix well with a fork until an almond meal mixture is formed.
5. Stir in vanilla and 1 tbsp. of cold water and mix until a firm dough is formed.
6. Cut the dough into two equal pieces and spread in a thin sheet.
7. Cut each sheet into 12 equal sized rectangles and transfer 4 rectangles in the Air fryer basket.
8. Cook for about 10 minutes and repeat with the remaining rectangles.
9. Lemon Glaze:
10. Meanwhile, mix all the ingredients for the lemon glaze and pour over the cooked tarts.
11. Top with sprinkles and serve.

Glazed Donuts

Servings: 2 – 4
Cooking Time: 25 Mins.

Ingredients:
- 1 can [8 oz.] refrigerated croissant dough
- Cooking spray
- 1 can [16 oz.] vanilla frosting

Directions:
1. Cut the croissant dough into 1-inch-round slices. Make a hole in the center of each one to create a donut.
2. Put the donuts in the Air Fryer basket, taking care not to overlap any, and spritz with cooking spray. You may need to cook everything in multiple batches.
3. Cook at 400°F for 2 minutes. Turn the donuts over and cook for another 3 minutes.
4. Place the rolls on a paper plate.
5. Microwave a half-cup of frosting for 30 seconds and pour a drizzling of the frosting over the donuts before serving.

Cherry-choco Bars

Servings: 8
Cooking Time: 15 Mins.

Ingredients:

- ¼ tsp. salt
- ½ cup almonds, sliced
- ½ cup chia seeds
- ½ cup dark chocolate, chopped
- ½ cup dried cherries, chopped
- ½ cup prunes, pureed
- ½ cup quinoa, cooked
- ¾ cup almond butter
- 1/3 cup honey
- 2 cups old-fashioned oats
- 2 tbsp. coconut oil

Directions:

1. Preheat the air fryer to 375oF.
2. In a mixing bowl, combine the oats, quinoa, chia seeds, almond, cherries, and chocolate.
3. In a saucepan, heat the almond butter, honey, and coconut oil.
4. Pour the butter mixture over the dry mixture. Add salt and prunes.
5. Mix until well combined.
6. Pour over a baking dish that can fit inside the air fryer.
7. Cook for 15 minutes.
8. Let it cool for an hour before slicing into bars.

Orange Muffins

Servings: 5
Cooking Time: 10 Mins.

Ingredients:

- 5 eggs, beaten
- 1 tbsp. poppy seeds
- 1 tsp. vanilla extract
- ¼ tsp. ground nutmeg
- ½ tsp. baking powder
- 1 tsp. orange juice
- 1 tsp. orange zest, grated
- 5 tbsps. coconut flour
- 1 tbsp. Monk fruit
- 2 tbsps. coconut flakes
- Cooking spray

Directions:

1. In the mixing bowl mix up eggs, poppy seeds, vanilla extract, ground nutmeg, baking powder, orange juice, orange zest, coconut flour, and Monk fruit. Add coconut flakes and mix up the mixture until it is homogenous and without any clumps. Preheat the air fryer to 360F. Spray the muffin molds with cooking spray from inside. Pour the muffin batter in the molds and transfer them in the air fryer. Cook the muffins for 10 minutes.

Layered Cake

Servings: 8
Cooking Time: 25 Mins.

Ingredients:
- For Cake:
- 3½ ozs. plain flour
- 1 tsp. ground cinnamon
- Pinch of salt
- 7 tbsps. sugar
- 3½ ozs. butter, softened
- 2 medium eggs
- For Filling:
- 1¾ ozs. butter, softened
- 1 tbsp. whipped cream
- 2/3 cup icing sugar
- 2 tbsps. strawberry jam

Directions:
1. In a large bowl, mix well flour, cinnamon, and salt.
2. In another bowl, add the sugar, and butter and whisk until creamy.
3. Add in the eggs and whisk until well combined.
4. Slowly, add the flour mixture whisking continuously until well combined
5. Set the temperature of air fryer to 355 degrees F. Grease a cake pan.
6. Place mixture evenly into the prepared cake pan.
7. Air fry for about 15 minutes and then, another 10 minutes at 335 degrees F.
8. Remove the cake pan from air fryer and place onto a wire rack to cool for about 10 minutes.
9. Now, invert the cake onto wire rack to completely cool before filling.
10. After cooling, cut the cake into 2 equal-sized portions.
11. For filling: in a bowl, add the butter and whisk until creamy.
12. Add the cream, and icing sugar and whisk until a thick creamy mixture forms.
13. Place one cake portion onto a serving platter, cut side up.
14. Spread the jam evenly over cake and top with butter mixture.
15. Arrange another cake over filling, cut side down.
16. Cut the cake into desired size slices and serve.

Hazelnut Brownie Cups

Servings: 12
Cooking Time: 30 Mins.

Ingredients:
- 6 oz. semisweet chocolate chips
- 1 stick butter, at room temperature
- 1 cup sugar
- 2 large eggs
- ¼ cup red wine
- ¼ tsp. hazelnut extract
- 1 tsp. pure vanilla extract
- ¾ cup flour
- 2 tbsp. cocoa powder
- ½ cup ground hazelnuts
- Pinch of kosher salt

Directions:
1. Melt the butter and chocolate chips in the microwave.
2. In a large bowl, combine the sugar, eggs, red wine, hazelnut and vanilla extract with a whisk. Pour in the chocolate mix.
3. Add in the flour, cocoa powder, ground hazelnuts, and a pinch of kosher salt, continuing to stir until a creamy, smooth consistency is achieved.
4. Take a muffin tin and place a cupcake liner in each cup. Spoon an equal amount of the batter into each one.
5. Air bake at 360°F for 28 - 30 minutes, cooking in batches if necessary.
6. Serve with a topping of ganache if desired.

Swirled German Cake

Servings: 8
Cooking Time: 25 Mins.

Ingredients:

- 1 cup flour
- 1 tsp. baking powder
- 1 cup sugar
- 1/8 tsp. kosher salt
- ¼ tsp. ground cinnamon
- ¼ tsp. grated nutmeg
- 1 tsp. orange zest
- 1 stick butter, melted
- 2 eggs
- 1 tsp. pure vanilla extract
- ¼ cup milk
- 2 tbsp. unsweetened cocoa powder

Directions:

1. Take a round pan that is small enough to fit inside your Air Fryer and lightly grease the inside with oil.
2. In a bowl, use an electric mixer to combine the flour, baking powder, sugar, salt, cinnamon, nutmeg, and orange zest.
3. Fold in the butter, eggs, vanilla, and milk, incorporating everything well.
4. Spoon a quarter-cup of the batter to the baking pan.
5. Stir the cocoa powder into the rest of the batter.
6. Use a spoon to drop small amounts of the brown batter into the white batter. Swirl them together with a knife.
7. Place the pan in the Air Fryer and cook at 360°F for about 15 minutes.
8. Remove the pan from the fryer and leave to cool for roughly 10 minutes.

Lemon Berry Jam

Servings: 12
Cooking Time: 20 Mins.

Ingredients:
- ¼ cup swerve
- 8 ozs. strawberries, sliced
- 1 tbsp. lemon juice
- ¼ cup water

Directions:
1. In a pan that fits the air fryer, combine all the ingredients, put the pan in the machine and cook at 380 degrees F for 20 minutes. Divide the mix into cups, cool down and serve.

Red Velvet Cupcakes

Servings: 12
Cooking Time: 12 Mins.

Ingredients:
- For Cupcakes:
- 2 cups refined flour
- ¾ cup peanut butter
- 3 eggs
- For Frosting:
- 1 cup butter
- 1 cup cream cheese
- For Cupcakes:
- ¾ cup icing sugar
- 2 tsps. beet powder
- 1 tsp. cocoa powder
- For Frosting:
- ¾ cup icing sugar
- ¼ cup strawberry sauce
- 1 tsp. vanilla essence

Directions:
1. Preheat the Air fryer to 340 F and grease 12 silicon cups lightly.
2. For cupcakes:
3. Mix all the ingredients in a large bowl until well combined.
4. Transfer the mixture into silicon cups and place in the Air fryer basket.
5. Cook for about 12 minutes and dish out.
6. For Frosting:
7. Mix all the ingredients in a large bowl until well combined.
8. Top each cupcake evenly with frosting and serve.

Berry Pie

Servings: 8
Cooking Time: 20 Mins.

Ingredients:
- 5 egg whites
- 1/3 cup swerve
- 1 and ½ cups almond flour
- Zest of 1 lemon, grated
- 1 tsp. baking powder
- 1 tsp. vanilla extract
- 1/3 cup butter, melted
- 2 cups strawberries, sliced
- Cooking spray

Directions:
1. In a bowl, whisk egg whites well. Add the rest of the ingredients except the cooking spray gradually and whisk everything. Grease a tart pan with the cooking spray, and pour the strawberries mix. Put the pan in the air fryer and cook at 370 degrees F for 20 minutes. Cool down, slice and serve.

BEEF, PORK & LAMB RECIPES

Roasted Ribeye Steak with Rum

Servings: 4
Cooking Time: 50 Mins.

Ingredients:

- ½ cup rum
- 2 lbs. bone-in ribeye steak
- 2 tbsps. extra virgin olive oil
- Salt and black pepper to taste

Directions:

1. Place all Ingredients in a Ziploc bag and allow to marinate in the fridge for at least 2 hours.
2. Preheat the air fryer to 390oF.
3. Place the grill pan accessory in the air fryer.
4. Grill for 25 minutes per piece.
5. Halfway through the cooking time, flip the meat for even grilling.

Shepherd's Pie Made of Ground Lamb

Servings: 4
Cooking Time: 50 Mins.

Ingredients:

- 1-pound lean ground lamb
- 2 tbsps. and 2 tsps. all-purpose flour
- salt and ground black pepper to taste
- 1 tsp. minced fresh rosemary
- 2 tbsps. cream cheese
- 2 ozs. Irish cheese (such as Dubliner®), shredded
- salt and ground black pepper to taste
- 1 tbsp. milk
- 1-1/2 tsps. olive oil
- 1-1/2 tsps. butter
- 1/2 onion, diced
- 1/2 tsp. paprika
- 1-1/2 tsps. ketchup
- 1-1/2 cloves garlic, minced
- 1/2 (12 ounce) package frozen peas and carrots, thawed
- 1-1/2 tsps. butter
- 1/2 pinch ground cayenne pepper
- 1/2 egg yolk
- 1-1/4 cups water, or as needed
- 1-1/4 lbs. Yukon Gold potatoes, peeled and halved
- 1/8 tsp. ground cinnamon

Directions:

1. Bring a large pan of salted water to boil and add potatoes. Simmer for 15 minutes until tender.
2. Meanwhile, lightly grease baking pan of air fryer with butter. Melt for 2 minutes at 3600F.
3. Add ground lamb and onion. Cook for 10 minutes, stirring and crumbling halfway through cooking time.
4. Add garlic, ketchup, cinnamon, paprika, rosemary, black pepper, salt, and flour. Mix well and cook for 3 minutes.
5. Add water and deglaze pan. Continue cooking for 6 minutes.
6. Stir in carrots and peas. Evenly spread mixture in pan.
7. Once potatoes are done, drain well and transfer potatoes to a bowl. Mash potatoes and stir in Irish cheese, cream cheese, cayenne pepper, and butter. Mix well. Season with pepper and salt to taste.

8. In a small bowl, whisk well milk and egg yolk. Stir into mashed potatoes.
9. Top the ground lamb mixture with mashed potatoes.
10. Cook for another 15 minutes or until tops of potatoes are lightly browned.
11. Serve and enjoy.

Grilled Tri Tip Over Beet Salad

Servings: 6
Cooking Time: 45 Mins.

Ingredients:
- 1 bunch arugula, torn
- 1 bunch scallions, chopped
- 1-pound tri-tip, sliced
- 2 tbsps. olive oil
- 3 beets, peeled and sliced thinly
- 3 tbsps. balsamic vinegar
- Salt and pepper to taste

Directions:
1. Preheat the air fryer to 390oF.
2. Place the grill pan accessory in the air fryer.
3. Season the tri-tip with salt and pepper. Drizzle with oil.
4. Grill for 15 minutes per batch.
5. Meanwhile, prepare the salad by tossing the rest of the ingredients in a salad bowl.
6. Toss in the grilled tri-trip and drizzle with more balsamic vinegar.

Leftover Beef and Kale Omelet

Servings: 4
Cooking Time: 20 Mins.

Ingredients:
- Non-stick cooking spray
- 1/2 lb. leftover beef, coarsely chopped
- 2 garlic cloves, pressed
- 1 cup kale, torn into pieces and wilted
- 1 tomato, chopped
- 1/4 tsp. brown sugar
- 4 eggs, beaten
- 4 tbsps. heavy cream
- 1/2 tsp. turmeric powder
- Salt and ground black pepper, to your liking
- 1/8 tsp. ground allspice

Directions:
1. Spritz the inside of four ramekins with a cooking spray.
2. Divide all of the above ingredients among the prepared ramekins. Stir until everything is well combined.
3. Air-fry at 360 degrees F for 16 minutes; check with a wooden stick and return the eggs to the Air Fryer for a few more minutes as needed. Serve immediately.

Pork with Balsamic-raspberry Jam

Servings: 4
Cooking Time: 30 Mins.

Ingredients:

- ¼ cup all-purpose flour
- ¼ cup milk
- 1 cup chopped pecans
- 1 cup panko breadcrumbs
- 2 large eggs, beaten
- 2 tbsps. raspberry jam
- 2 tbsps. sugar
- 2/3 cup balsamic vinegar
- 4 smoked pork chops
- Salt and pepper to taste

Directions:

1. Preheat the air fryer to 3300F.
2. Season pork chops with salt and pepper to taste.
3. In a small bowl, whisk together eggs and milk. Set aside.
4. Dip the pork chops in flour then in the egg mixture before dredging in the panko mixed with pecans.
5. Place in the air fryer and cook for 30 minutes.
6. Meanwhile, prepare the sauce by putting in the saucepan the remaining Ingredients. Season with salt and pepper.
7. Drizzle the pork chops with the sauce once cooked.

Peppermint Lamb

Servings: 4
Cooking Time: 12 Mins.

Ingredients:
- 1-pound lamb chops
- 2 oz celery ribs, chopped
- ½ tsp. lemon zest, grated
- ½ tsp. garlic, minced
- ½ tsp. peppermint
- 1 tbsp. ghee
- ½ tsp. ground black pepper
- 1 tsp. olive oil

Directions:
1. Put the celery ribs in the blender. Add lemon zest, garlic, peppermint, ghee, ground black pepper, and olive oil. Pulse the mixture for 1-2 minutes. Then carefully rub the lamb chops with blended mixture and put the meat in the air fryer. Cook the lamb chops for 6 minutes from each side at 400F.

Beef Bulgogi

Servings: 1

Cooking Time: 15 Mins.

Ingredients:
- ½ cup sliced mushrooms
- 2 tbsp bulgogi marinade
- 1 tbsp diced onion

Directions:
1. Cut the beef into small pieces and place them in a bowl. Add the bulgogi and mix to coat the beef completely. Cover the bowl and place in the fridge for 3 hours. Preheat the air fryer to 350 F.
2. Transfer the beef to a baking dish; stir in the mushroom and onion. Cook for 10 minutes, until nice and tender. Serve with some roasted potatoes and a green salad.

Family Pork Loin Roast

Servings: 6
Cooking Time: 55 Mins.

Ingredients:
- 1 ½ lbs. boneless pork loin roast, washed
- 1 tsp. mustard seeds
- 1 tsp. garlic powder
- 1 tsp. porcini powder
- 1 tsp. shallot powder
- 3/4 tsp. sea salt flakes
- 1 tsp. red pepper flakes, crushed
- 2 dried sprigs thyme, crushed
- 2 tbsps. lime juice

Directions:
1. Firstly, score the meat using a small knife; make sure to not cut too deep.
2. In a small-sized mixing dish, combine all seasonings in the order listed above; mix to combine well.
3. Massage the spice mix into the pork meat to evenly distribute. Drizzle with lemon juice.
4. Then, set your Air Fryer to cook at 360 degrees F. Place the pork in the Air Fryer basket; roast for 25 to 30 minutes. Pause the machine, check for doneness and cook for 25 minutes more.

Bbq Skirt Steak

Servings: 5
Cooking Time: 20 Mins. + Marinating Time

Ingredients:
- 2 lbs. skirt steak
- 2 tbsps. tomato paste
- 1 tbsp. olive oil
- 1 tbsp. coconut aminos
- 1/4 cup rice vinegar
- 1 tbsp. fish sauce
- Sea salt, to taste
- 1/2 tsp. dried dill
- 1/2 tsp. dried rosemary
- 1/4 tsp. black pepper, freshly cracked

Directions:
1. Place all ingredients in a large ceramic dish; let it marinate for 3 hours in your refrigerator.
2. Coat the sides and bottom of the Air Fryer with cooking spray.
3. Add your steak to the cooking basket; reserve the marinade. Cook the skirt steak in the preheated Air Fryer at 400 degrees F for 12 minutes, turning over a couple of times, basting with the reserved marinade.
4. Bon appétit!

Spicy Lamb Kebabs

Servings: 6
Cooking Time: 8 Mins.

Ingredients:
- 4 eggs, beaten
- 1 cup pistachios, chopped
- 1 lb. ground lamb
- 4 tbsps. plain flour
- 4 tbsps. flat-leaf parsley, chopped
- 2 tsps. chili flakes
- 4 garlic cloves, minced
- 2 tbsps. fresh lemon juice
- 2 tsps. cumin seeds
- 1 tsp. fennel seeds
- 2 tsps. dried mint
- 2 tsps. salt
- Olive oil
- 1 tsp. coriander seeds
- 1 tsp. freshly ground black pepper

Directions:
1. Preheat the Air fryer to 355 F and grease an Air fryer basket.
2. Mix lamb, pistachios, eggs, lemon juice, chili flakes, flour, cumin seeds, fennel seeds, coriander seeds, mint, parsley, salt and black pepper in a large bowl.
3. Thread the lamb mixture onto metal skewers to form sausages and coat with olive oil.
4. Place the skewers in the Air fryer basket and cook for about 8 minutes.
5. Dish out in a platter and serve hot.

Hot Paprika Beef

Servings: 4
Cooking Time: 20 Mins.

Ingredients:

- 1 tbsp. hot paprika
- 4 beef steaks
- Salt and black pepper to the taste
- 1 tbsp. butter, melted

Directions:

1. In a bowl, mix the beef with the rest of the ingredients, rub well, transfer the steaks to your air fryer's basket and cook at 390 degrees F for 10 minutes on each side. Divide the steaks between plates and serve with a side salad.

POULTRY RECIPES

Bbq Pineapple 'n Teriyaki Glazed Chicken

Servings: 4
Cooking Time: 23 Mins.

Ingredients:
- ¼ cup pineapple juice
- ¼ tsp. pepper
- ½ cup brown sugar
- ½ cup soy sauce
- ½ tsp. salt
- 1 green bell pepper, cut into 1-inch cubes
- 1 red bell pepper, cut into 1-inch cubes
- 1 red onion, cut into 1-inch cubes
- 1 tbsp. cornstarch
- 1 tbsp. water
- 1 yellow red bell pepper, cut into 1-inch cubes
- 2 boneless skinless chicken breasts, cut into 1-inch cubes
- 2 cups fresh pineapple cut into 1-inch cubes
- 2 garlic cloves, minced
- green onions, for garnish

Directions:
1. In a saucepan, bring to a boil salt, pepper, garlic, pineapple juice, soy sauce, and brown sugar. In a small bowl whisk well, cornstarch and water. Slowly stir in to mixture in pan while whisking constantly. Simmer until thickened, around 3 minutes. Save ¼ cup of the sauce for basting and set aside.
2. In shallow dish, mix well chicken and remaining thickened sauce. Toss well to coat. Marinate in the ref for a half hour.
3. Thread bell pepper, onion, pineapple, and chicken pieces in skewers. Place on skewer rack in air fryer.
4. For 10 minutes, cook on 360oF. Halfway through cooking time, turnover skewers and baste with sauce. If needed, cook in batches.
5. Serve and enjoy with a sprinkle of green onions.

Turkey Loaf

Servings: 4
Cooking Time: 50 Mins.

Ingredients:
- 2/3 cup of finely chopped walnuts
- 1 egg
- 1 tbsp. organic tomato paste
- 1 ½ lb. turkey breast, diced
- 1 tbsp. Dijon mustard
- ½ tsp. dried savory or dill
- 1 tbsp. onion flakes
- ½ tsp. ground allspice
- 1 small garlic clove, minced
- ½ tsp. sea salt
- ¼ tsp. black pepper
- 1 tbsp. liquid aminos
- 2 tbsp. grated parmesan cheese

Directions:
1. Pre-heat Air Fryer to 375°F.
2. Coat the inside of a baking dish with a little oil.
3. Mix together the egg, dill, tomato paste, liquid aminos, mustard, salt, dill, garlic, pepper and allspice using a whisk. Stir in the diced turkey, followed by the walnuts, cheese and onion flakes.
4. Transfer the mixture to the greased baking dish and bake in the Air Fryer for 40 minutes.
5. Serve hot.

Tangy Chicken with Parsley and Lime

Servings: 2
Cooking Time: 30 Mins. + Marinating Time

Ingredients:

- 1 1/2 handful fresh parsley, roughly chopped
- Fresh juice of 1/2 lime
- 1 tsp. ground black pepper
- 1 1/2 large-sized chicken breasts, cut into halves
- 1 tsp. kosher salt
- Zest of 1/2 lime

Directions:

1. Preheat your Air Fryer to 335 degrees F.
2. Toss the chicken breasts with the other ingredients and let it marinate a couple of hours.
3. Roast for 26 minutes and serve warm. Bon appétit!

Sausage, Ham and Hash Brown Bake

Servings: 4
Cooking Time: 45 Mins.

Ingredients:

- 1/2 lb. chicken sausages, smoked
- 1/2 lb. ham, sliced
- 6 ozs. hash browns, frozen and shredded
- 2 garlic cloves, minced
- 8 ozs. spinach
- 1/2 cup Ricotta cheese
- 1/2 cup Asiago cheese, grated
- 4 eggs
- 1/2 cup yogurt
- 1/2 cup milk
- Salt and ground black pepper, to taste
- 1 tsp. smoked paprika

Directions:

1. Start by preheating your Air Fryer to 380 degrees F. Cook the sausages and ham for 10 minutes; set aside.
2. Meanwhile, in a preheated saucepan, cook the hash browns and garlic for 4 minutes, stirring frequently; remove from the heat, add the spinach and cover with the lid.
3. Allow the spinach to wilt completely. Transfer the sautéed mixture to a baking pan. Add the reserved sausage and ham.
4. In a mixing dish, thoroughly combine the cheese, eggs, yogurt, milk, salt, pepper, and paprika. Pour the cheese mixture over the hash browns in the pan.
5. Place the baking pan in the cooking basket and cook approximately 30 minutes or until everything is thoroughly cooked. Bon appétit!

Quick 'n Easy Garlic Herb Wings

Servings: 4
Cooking Time: 35 Mins.

Ingredients:
- ¼ cup chopped rosemary
- 2 lbs. chicken wings
- 6 medium garlic cloves , grated
- Salt and pepper to taste

Directions:
1. Season the chicken with garlic, rosemary, salt and pepper.
2. Preheat the air fryer to 3900F.
3. Place the grill pan accessory in the air fryer.
4. Grill for 35 minutes and make sure to flip the chicken every 10 minutes.

Lebanese Style Grilled Chicken

Servings: 3
Cooking Time: 20 Mins.

Ingredients:

- 1 onion, cut into large chunks
- 1 small green bell pepper, cut into large chunks
- 1 tsp. tomato paste
- 1/2 cup chopped fresh flat-leaf parsley
- 1/2 tsp. dried oregano
- 1/3 cup plain yogurt
- 1/8 tsp. ground allspice
- 1/8 tsp. ground black pepper
- 1/8 tsp. ground cardamom
- 1/8 tsp. ground cinnamon
- 1-pound skinless, boneless chicken breast halves cut into 2-inch pieces
- 2 cloves garlic, minced
- 2 tbsps. lemon juice
- 2 tbsps. vegetable oil
- 3/4 tsp. salt

Directions:

1. In a resealable plastic bag, mix cardamom, cinnamon, allspice, pepper, oregano, salt, tomato paste, garlic, yogurt, vegetable oil, and lemon juice. Add chicken, remove excess air, seal, and marinate in the ref for at least 4 hours.
2. Thread chicken into skewers, place on skewer rack and cook in batches.
3. For 10 minutes, cook on 3600F. Halfway through cooking time, turnover skewers.
4. Serve and enjoy with a sprinkle of parsley.

Chicken Egg Rolls with Hot Dipping Sauce

Servings: 5
Cooking Time: 35 Mins.

Ingredients:
- 2 tsps. olive oil
- 1 lb. ground chicken
- Salt and ground pepper, to taste
- 2 scallions, sliced thinly
- 2 cloves garlic, finely chopped
- 2 cups Napa cabbage, shredded
- 2 tbsps. soy sauce
- 1 tsp. Dijon mustard
- 10 egg roll wrappers
- Dipping Sauce:
- 1/3 cup lite soy sauce
- 1/3 cup Champagne vinegar
- 2 tbsps. molasses
- 1 tbsp. sesame oil
- 1/2 tsp. chili powder

Directions:
1. In a cast-iron skillet, heat the oil until sizzling; now, add the ground chicken and cook for 3 to 4 minutes, crumbling with a fork. Season with salt and pepper.
2. Stir in the scallions, garlic, and cabbage. Continue to sauté for 4 minutes more. Remove from the heat; add the soy sauce and mustard and stir again.
3. Fill the egg roll wrappers, using 1 to 2 tbsps. of filling. Place the filling in the center of the wrapper. Roll the corner over the filling and brush it with water.
4. Fold in the sides of the wrapper and continue rolling until it is closed. Press to seal and brush it with water.
5. Cook in the preheated Air Fryer at 375 degrees F for 13 to 16 minutes, turning over halfway through. Work in batches.
6. In the meantime, combine all of the sauce ingredients in a mixing bowl. Serve immediately with the warm egg rolls.

Fried Chicken Legs

Servings: 5
Cooking Time: 50 Mins.

Ingredients:
- 2 lemons, halved
- 5 tbsp garlic powder
- 5 tbsp oregano, dried
- ⅓ cup olive oil
- Salt and black pepper

Directions:
1. Set air fryer to 350 F. Brush the chicken legs with some olive oil.
2. Sprinkle with the lemon juice and arrange on the air fryer basket. In another bowl, combine, oregano, garlic powder, salt and pepper. Sprinkle the seasoning mixture over the chicken. Cook in the air fryer for 20 minutes, shaking every 5 minutes.

Crispy Chicken Thighs

Servings: 1
Cooking Time: 35 Mins.

Ingredients:
- 1 lb. chicken thighs
- Salt and pepper
- 2 cups roasted pecans
- 1 cup water
- 1 cup flour

Directions:
1. Pre-heat your fryer to 400°F.
2. Season the chicken with salt and pepper, then set aside.
3. Pulse the roasted pecans in a food processor until a flour-like consistency is achieved.
4. Fill a dish with the water, another with the flour, and a third with the pecans.
5. Coat the thighs with the flour. Mix the remaining flour with the processed pecans.
6. Dredge the thighs in the water and then press into the -pecan mix, ensuring the chicken is completely covered.
7. Cook the chicken in the fryer for twenty-two minutes, with an extra five minutes added if you would like the chicken a darker-brown color. Check the temperature has reached 165°F before serving.

Lemon-oregano Chicken Bbq

Servings: 6
Cooking Time: 40 Mins.

Ingredients:
- 1 tbsp. grated lemon zest
- 2 tbsps. fresh lemon juice
- 2 tbsps. oregano, chopped
- 3 lbs. chicken breasts
- 4 cloves of garlic, minced
- Salt and pepper to taste

Directions:
1. Preheat the air fryer to 390oF.
2. Place the grill pan accessory in the air fryer.
3. Season the chicken with oregano, garlic, lemon zest, lemon juice, salt and pepper.
4. Grill for 40 minutes and flip every 10 minutes to cook evenly.

Easy Turkey Breasts with Basil

Servings: 4
Cooking Time: 1 Hour

Ingredients:
- 2 tbsps. olive oil
- 2 lbs. turkey breasts, bone-in skin-on
- Coarse sea salt and ground black pepper, to taste
- 1 tsp. fresh basil leaves, chopped
- 2 tbsps. lemon zest, grated

Directions:
1. Rub olive oil on all sides of the turkey breasts; sprinkle with salt, pepper, basil, and lemon zest.
2. Place the turkey breasts skin side up on a parchment-lined cooking basket.
3. Cook in the preheated Air Fryer at 330 degrees F for 30 minutes. Now, turn them over and cook an additional 28 minutes.
4. Serve with lemon wedges, if desired. Bon appétit!

Lime and Mustard Marinated Chicken

Servings: 4

Cooking Time: 30 Mins. + Marinating Time

Ingredients:

- 1/2 tsp. stone-ground mustard
- 1/2 tsp. minced fresh oregano
- 1/3 cup freshly squeezed lime juice
- 2 small-sized chicken breasts, skin-on
- 1 tsp. kosher salt
- 1teaspoon freshly cracked mixed peppercorns

Directions:

1. Preheat your Air Fryer to 345 degrees F.
2. Toss all of the above ingredients in a medium-sized mixing dish; allow it to marinate overnight.
3. Cook in the preheated Air Fryer for 26 minutes. Bon appétit!

FISH & SEAFOOD RECIPES

Wrapped Scallops

Servings: 4
Cooking Time: 7 Mins.

Ingredients:
- 1 tsp. ground coriander
- ½ tsp. ground paprika
- ¼ tsp. salt
- 16 oz scallops
- 4 oz bacon, sliced
- 1 tsp. sesame oil

Directions:
1. Sprinkle the scallops with ground coriander, ground paprika, and salt. Then wrap the scallops in the bacon slices and secure with toothpicks. Sprinkle the scallops with sesame oil. Preheat the air fryer to 400F. Put the scallops in the air fryer basket and cook them for 7 minutes.

Juicy Salmon and Asparagus Parcels

Servings: 2
Cooking Time: 13 Mins.

Ingredients:
- 2 salmon fillets
- 4 asparagus stalks
- ¼ cup champagne
- Salt and black pepper, to taste
- ¼ cup white sauce
- 1 tsp. olive oil

Directions:
1. Preheat the Air fryer to 355 F and grease an Air fryer basket.
2. Mix all the ingredients in a bowl and divide this mixture evenly over 2 foil papers.
3. Arrange the foil papers in the Air fryer basket and cook for about 13 minutes.
4. Dish out in a platter and serve hot.

Tuna Stuffed Avocado

Servings: 2
Cooking Time: 12 Mins.

Ingredients:
- 1 avocado, pitted, halved
- ½ lb. smoked tuna, boneless and shredded
- 1 egg, beaten
- ½ tsp. salt
- ½ tsp. chili powder
- ½ tsp. ground nutmeg
- 1 tsp. dried parsley
- Cooking spray

Directions:
1. Scoop ½ part of the avocado meat from the avocado to get the avocado boats. Use the scooper for this step. After this, in the mixing bowl mix up tuna and egg. Shred the mixture with the help of the fork. Add salt, chili powder, ground nutmeg, and dried parsley. Stir the tuna mixture until homogenous. Add the scooped avocado meat and mix up the mixture well. Fill the avocado boats with tuna mixture. Preheat the air fryer to 385F. Arrange the tuna boats in the air fryer basket and cook them for 12 minutes.

Bacon Wrapped Scallops

Servings: 4
Cooking Time: 12 Mins.

Ingredients:
- 5 center-cut bacon slices, cut each in 4 pieces
- 20 sea scallops, cleaned and patted very dry
- Olive oil cooking spray
- 1 tsp. lemon pepper seasoning
- ½ tsp. paprika
- Salt and ground black pepper, to taste

Directions:
1. Preheat the Air fryer to 400 F and grease an Air fryer basket.
2. Wrap each scallop with a piece of bacon and secure each with a toothpick.
3. Season the scallops evenly with lemon pepper seasoning and paprika.
4. Arrange half of the scallops into the Air fryer basket and spray with cooking spray.
5. Season with salt and black pepper and cook for about 6 minutes.
6. Repeat with the remaining half and serve warm.

Spicy Prawns

Servings: 2
Cooking Time: 8 Mins.

Ingredients:

- 6 prawns
- 1/4 tsp pepper
- 1/2 tsp chili powder
- 1 tsp chili flakes
- 1/4 tsp salt

Directions:

1. Preheat the air fryer to 350 F.
2. In a bowl, mix together spices add prawns.
3. Spray air fryer basket with cooking spray.
4. Transfer prawns into the air fryer basket and cook for 8 minutes.
5. Serve and enjoy.

Fennel Salad Topped with Roast Salmon

Servings: 4

Cooking Time: 10 Mins.

Ingredients:

- 1 clove of garlic, grated
- 1 tsp. fresh thyme, chopped
- 1 tsp. salt
- 2 tbsps. chopped dill
- 2 tbsps. olive oil
- 2 tbsps. orange juice
- 2 tsps. chopped parsley
- 2/3 cup Greek yogurt
- 4 pieces salmon fillets
- 4 cups sliced fennel

Directions:

1. Preheat the air fryer to 3900F.
2. Season the salmon fillets with parsley, thyme, salt, and olive oil. Rub the spices on the salon.
3. Place the grill pan accessory in the air fryer.
4. Place the fish and cook for 10 minutes.
5. Flip the fish halfway through the cooking time to brown all sides evenly.
6. While the fish is cooking, prepare the salad by combining the rest of the rest of the ingredients in a bowl.
7. Serve the fish with the salad.

Creamed Trout Salad

Servings: 2
Cooking Time: 20 Mins.

Ingredients:
- 1/2 lb. trout fillets, skinless
- 2 tbsps. horseradish, prepared, drained
- 1/4 cup mayonnaise
- 1 tbsp. fresh lemon juice
- 1 tsp. mustard
- Salt and ground white pepper, to taste
- 6 ozs. chickpeas, canned and drained
- 1 red onion, thinly sliced
- 1 cup Iceberg lettuce, torn into pieces

Directions:
1. Spritz the Air Fryer basket with cooking spray.
2. Cook the trout fillets in the preheated Air Fryer at 395 degrees F for 10 minutes or until opaque. Make sure to turn them halfway through the cooking time.
3. Break the fish into bite-sized chunks and place in the refrigerator to cool. Toss your fish with the remaining ingredients. Bon appétit!

Butter Paprika Swordfish

Servings: 4
Cooking Time: 12 Mins.

Ingredients:

- 4 swordfish fillets, boneless
- 1 tbsp. olive oil
- ¾ tsp. sweet paprika
- 2 tsps. basil, dried
- Juice of 1 lemon
- 2 tbsps. butter, melted

Directions:

1. In a bowl, mix the oil with the other ingredients except the fish fillets and whisk. Brush the fish with this mix, place it in your air fryer's basket and cook for 6 minutes on each side. Divide between plates and serve with a side salad.

Glazed Halibut Steak

Servings: 3
Cooking Time: 70 Mins.

Ingredients:
- 1 lb. halibut steak
- 2/3 cup low-sodium soy sauce
- ½ cup mirin
- 2 tbsp. lime juice
- ¼ cup sugar
- ¼ tsp. crushed red pepper flakes
- ¼ cup orange juice
- 1 garlic clove, smashed
- ¼ tsp. ginger, ground

Directions:
1. 1 Make the teriyaki glaze by mixing together all of the ingredients except for the halibut in a saucepan.
2. 2 Bring it to a boil and lower the heat, stirring constantly until the mixture reduces by half. Remove from the heat and leave to cool.
3. 3 Pour half of the cooled glaze into a Ziploc bag. Add in the halibut, making sure to coat it well in the sauce. Place in the refrigerator for 30 minutes.
4. 4 Pre-heat the Air Fryer to 390°F.
5. 5 Put the marinated halibut in the fryer and allow to cook for 10 – 12 minutes.
6. 6 Use any the remaining glaze to lightly brush the halibut steak with.
7. 7 Serve with white rice or shredded vegetables.

Pollock with Kalamata Olives and Capers

Servings: 3
Cooking Time: 20 Mins.

Ingredients:

- 2 tbsps. olive oil
- 1 red onion, sliced
- 2 cloves garlic, chopped
- 1 Florina pepper, deveined and minced
- 3 pollock fillets, skinless
- 2 ripe tomatoes, diced
- 12 Kalamata olives, pitted and chopped
- 2 tbsps. capers
- 1 tsp. oregano
- 1 tsp. rosemary
- Sea salt, to taste
- 1/2 cup white wine

Directions:

1. Start by preheating your Air Fryer to 360 degrees F. Heat the oil in a baking pan. Once hot, sauté the onion, garlic, and pepper for 2 to 3 minutes or until fragrant.
2. Add the fish fillets to the baking pan. Top with the tomatoes, olives, and capers. Sprinkle with the oregano, rosemary, and salt. Pour in white wine and transfer to the cooking basket.
3. Turn the temperature to 395 degrees F and bake for 10 minutes. Taste for seasoning and serve on individual plates, garnished with some extra Mediterranean herbs if desired. Enjoy!

Shrimp Magic

Servings: 3
Cooking Time: 5 Mins.

Ingredients:

- 1½ lbs. shrimps, peeled and deveined
- Lemongrass stalks
- 4 garlic cloves, minced
- 1 red chili pepper, seeded and chopped
- 2 tbsps. olive oil
- ½ tsp. smoked paprika

Directions:

1. Preheat the Air fryer to 390 F and grease an Air fryer basket.
2. Mix all the ingredients in a large bowl and refrigerate to marinate for about 2 hours.
3. Thread the shrimps onto lemongrass stalks and transfer into the Air fryer basket.
4. Cook for about 5 minutes and dish out to serve warm.

SNACKS & APPETIZERS RECIPES

Sweet Corn and Bell Pepper Sandwich with Barbecue Sauce

Servings: 2
Cooking Time: 23 Mins.

Ingredients:
- 2 tbsps. butter, softened
- 1 cup sweet corn kernels
- 1 roasted green bell pepper, chopped
- 4 bread slices, trimmed and cut horizontally
- ¼ cup barbecue sauce

Directions:
1. Preheat the Air fryer to 355 F and grease an Air fryer basket.
2. Heat butter in a skillet on medium heat and add corn.
3. Sauté for about 2 minutes and dish out in a bowl.
4. Add bell pepper and barbecue sauce to the corn.
5. Spread corn mixture on one side of 2 bread slices and top with remaining slices.
6. Dish out and serve warm.

Sweet and Spicy Carrot Sticks

Servings: 2

Cooking Time: 12 Mins.

Ingredients:
- 1 large carrot, peeled and cut into sticks
- 1 tbsp. fresh rosemary, chopped finely
- 1 tbsp. olive oil
- 2 tsps. sugar
- ¼ tsp. cayenne pepper
- Salt and black pepper, to taste

Directions:
1. Preheat the Air fryer to 390 F and grease an Air fryer basket
2. Mix carrot with all other ingredients in a bowl until well combined.
3. Arrange the carrot sticks in the Air fryer basket and cook for about 12 minutes.
4. Dish out and serve warm.

Juicy Meatballs

Servings: 5
Cooking Time: 14 Mins.

Ingredients:
- 1 lb ground beef
- 1 tsp garlic powder
- 1 egg, lightly beaten
- 1/2 onion, diced
- 1/4 tsp pepper
- 1 tsp salt

Directions:
1. Spray air fryer basket with cooking spray.
2. Preheat the air fryer to 390 F.
3. Add all ingredients into the bowl and mix until well combined.
4. Make balls from meat mixture and place into the air fryer basket.
5. Cook meatballs for 14 minutes. Shake basket 3-4 times while cooking.
6. Serve and enjoy.

Bruschetta with Fresh Tomato and Basil

Servings: 3
Cooking Time: 15 Mins.

Ingredients:
- 1/2 Italian bread, sliced
- 2 garlic cloves, peeled
- 2 tbsps. extra-virgin olive oil
- 2 ripe tomatoes, chopped
- 1 tsp. dried oregano
- Salt, to taste
- 8 fresh basil leaves, roughly chopped

Directions:
1. Place the bread slices on the lightly greased Air Fryer grill pan. Bake at 370 degrees F for 3 minutes.
2. Cut a clove of garlic in half and rub over one side of the toast; brush with olive oil. Add the chopped tomatoes. Sprinkle with oregano and salt.
3. Increase the temperature to 380 degrees F. Cook in the preheated Air Fryer for 3 minutes more.
4. Garnish with fresh basil and serve. Bon appétit!

Spicy Broccoli Poppers

Servings: 4
Cooking Time: 10 Mins.

Ingredients:
- 2 tbsps. plain yogurt
- 1 lb. broccoli, cut into small florets
- 2 tbsps. chickpea flour
- ½ tsp. red chili powder
- ¼ tsp. ground cumin
- ¼ tsp. ground turmeric
- Salt, to taste

Directions:
1. Preheat the Air fryer to 400 F and grease an Air fryer basket.
2. Mix together the yogurt, red chili powder, cumin, turmeric and salt in a bowl until well combined.
3. Stir in the broccoli and generously coat with marinade.
4. Refrigerate for about 30 minutes and sprinkle the broccoli florets with chickpea flour.
5. Arrange the broccoli florets in the Air fryer basket and cook for about 10 minutes, flipping once in between.
6. Dish out and serve warm.

Crunchy Bacon Bites

Servings: 4
Cooking Time: 10 Mins.

Ingredients:
- 4 bacon strips, cut into small pieces
- 1/2 cup pork rinds, crushed
- 1/4 cup hot sauce

Directions:
1. Add bacon pieces in a bowl.
2. Add hot sauce and toss well.
3. Add crushed pork rinds and toss until bacon pieces are well coated.
4. Transfer bacon pieces in air fryer basket and cook at 350 F for 10 minutes.
5. Serve and enjoy.

Onion Rings

Servings: 2
Cooking Time: 25 Mins.

Ingredients:
- 1 large onion, cut into slices
- 1 egg, beaten
- ¾ cup friendly bread crumbs
- 1 cup milk
- 1 tsp. baking powder
- 1 ¼ cup flour
- 1 tsp. salt

Directions:
1. Pre-heat the Air Fryer for 5 minutes.
2. In a small bowl, combine the baking powder, flour, and salt
3. In a second bowl, stir together the milk and egg using a whisk.
4. Put the bread crumbs in a shallow dish.
5. Coat each slice of onion with the flour, then dredge it in the egg mixture. Lastly, press it into the breadcrumbs.
6. Transfer the coated onion rings to the Air Fryer basket and cook at
7. 350°F for 10 minutes.

Baked Tortillas

Servings: 4
Cooking Time: 30 Mins.

Ingredients:
- 1 large head of cauliflower divided into florets.
- 4 large eggs
- 2 garlic cloves (minced)
- 1 ½ tsp herbs (whatever your favorite is - basil, oregano, thyme)
- ½ tsp salt

Directions:
1. Preheat your fryer to 375°F/190°C.
2. Put parchment paper on two baking sheets.
3. In a food processor, break down the cauliflower into rice.
4. Add ¼ cup water and the riced cauliflower to a saucepan.
5. Cook on a medium high heat until tender for 10 minutes. Drain.
6. Dry with a clean kitchen towel.
7. Mix the cauliflower, eggs, garlic, herbs and salt.
8. Make 4 thin circles on the parchment paper.
9. Bake for 20 minutes, until dry.

Roasted Peppers

Servings: 4
Cooking Time: 40 Mins.

Ingredients:
- 12 medium bell peppers
- 1 sweet onion, small
- 1 tbsp. Maggi sauce
- 1 tbsp. extra virgin olive oil

Directions:
1. 1 Warm up the olive oil and Maggi sauce in Air Fryer at 320°F.
2. 2 Peel the onion, slice it into 1-inch pieces, and add it to the Air Fryer.
3. 3 Wash and de-stem the peppers. Slice them into 1-inch pieces and remove all the seeds, with water if necessary [ensuring to dry the peppers afterwards].
4. 4 Place the peppers in the Air Fryer.
5. 5 Cook for about 25 minutes, or longer if desired. Serve hot.

Garlic Potatoes

Servings: 4
Cooking Time: 40 Mins.

Ingredients:
- 1 lb. russet baking potatoes
- 1 tbsp. garlic powder
- 1 tbsp. freshly chopped parsley
- ½ tsp. salt
- ¼ tsp. black pepper
- 1 – 2 tbsp. olive oil

Directions:
1. Wash the potatoes and pat them dry with clean paper towels.
2. Pierce each potato several times with a fork.
3. Place the potatoes in a large bowl and season with the garlic powder, salt and pepper.
4. Pour over the olive oil and mix well.
5. Pre-heat the Air Fryer to 360°F.
6. Place the potatoes in the fryer and cook for about 30 minutes, shaking the basket a few times throughout the cooking time.
7. Garnish the potatoes with the chopped parsley and serve with butter, sour cream or another dipping sauce if desired.

Decadent Brie and Pork Meatballs

Servings: 8
Cooking Time: 25 Mins.

Ingredients:

- 1 tsp. cayenne pepper
- 2 tsps. mustard
- 2 tbsps. Brie cheese, grated
- 5 garlic cloves, minced
- 2 small-sized yellow onions, peeled and chopped
- 1½ lbs. ground pork
- Sea salt and freshly ground black pepper, to taste

Directions:

1. Mix all of the above ingredients until everything is well incorporated.
2. Now, form the mixture into balls (the size of golf a ball).
3. Cook for 17 minutes at 375 degrees F. Serve with your favorite sauce.

VEGAN & VEGETARIAN RECIPES

Roasted Pepper Salad with Goat Cheese

Servings: 4
Cooking Time: 20 Mins. + Chilling Time

Ingredients:
- 1 yellow bell pepper
- 1 red bell pepper
- 1 Serrano pepper
- 4 tbsps. olive oil
- 2 tbsps. cider vinegar
- 2 garlic cloves, peeled and pressed
- 1 tsp. cayenne pepper
- Sea salt, to taste
- 1/2 tsp. mixed peppercorns, freshly crushed
- 1/2 cup goat cheese, cubed
- 2 tbsps. fresh Italian parsley leaves, roughly chopped

Directions:
1. Start by preheating your Air Fryer to 400 degrees F. Brush the Air Fryer basket lightly with cooking oil.
2. Then, roast the peppers for 5 minutes. Give the peppers a half turn; place them back in the cooking basket and roast for another 5 minutes.
3. Turn them one more time and roast until the skin is charred and soft or 5 more minutes. Peel the peppers and let them cool to room temperature.
4. In a small mixing dish, whisk the olive oil, vinegar, garlic, cayenne pepper, salt, and crushed peppercorns. Dress the salad and set aside.
5. Scatter goat cheese over the peppers and garnish with parsley. Bon appétit!

Hasselback Potatoes

Servings: 4
Cooking Time: 30 Mins.

Ingredients:
- 4 potatoes
- 2 tbsps. Parmesan cheese, shredded
- 1 tbsp. fresh chives, chopped
- 2 tbsps. olive oil

Directions:
1. Preheat the Air fryer to 355 F and grease an Air fryer basket.
2. Cut slits along each potato about ¼-inch apart with a sharp knife, making sure slices should stay connected at the bottom.
3. Coat the potatoes with olive oil and arrange into the Air fryer basket.
4. Cook for about 30 minutes and dish out in a platter.
5. Top with chives and Parmesan cheese to serve.

Tangy Asparagus and Broccoli

Servings: 4
Cooking Time: 25 Mins.

Ingredients:
- 1/2 lb. asparagus, cut into 1 1/2-inch pieces
- 1/2 lb. broccoli, cut into 1 1/2-inch pieces
- 2 tbsps. peanut oil
- Some salt and white pepper, to taste
- 1/2 cup chicken broth
- 2 tbsps. apple cider vinegar

Directions:
1. Place the vegetables in a single layer in the lightly greased cooking basket. Drizzle the peanut oil over the vegetables.
2. Sprinkle with salt and white pepper.
3. Cook at 380 degrees F for 15 minutes, shaking the basket halfway through the cooking time.
4. Add 1/2 cup of chicken broth to a saucepan; bring to a rapid boil and add the vinegar. Cook for 5 to 7 minutes or until the sauce has reduced by half.
5. Spoon the sauce over the warm vegetables and serve immediately. Bon appétit!

Poblano & Tomato Stuffed Squash

Servings: 3
Cooking Time: 50 Mins.

Ingredients:
- 6 grape tomatoes, halved
- 1 poblano pepper, cut into strips
- ¼ cup grated mozzarella, optional
- 2 tsp olive oil divided
- Salt and pepper, to taste

Directions:
1. Preheat the air fryer to 350 F. Trim the ends and cut the squash lengthwise. You will only need one half for this recipe Scoop the flash out, so you make room for the filling. Brush 1 tsp of oil over the squash.
2. Place in the air fryer and roast for 30 minutes. Combine the remaining olive oil with tomatoes and poblanos, season with salt and pepper. Place the peppers and tomatoes into the squash. Cook for 15 more minutes. If using mozzarella, add it on top of the squash, two minutes before the end.

Baked Spicy Tortilla Chips

Servings: 3
Cooking Time: 20 Mins.

Ingredients:

- 6 (6-inch) corn tortillas
- 1 tsp. canola oil
- 1 tsp. salt
- 1/4 tsp. ground white pepper
- 1/2 tsp. ground cumin
- 1/2 tsp. ancho chili powder

Directions:

1. Slice the tortillas into quarters. Brush the tortilla pieces with the canola oil until well coated.
2. Toss with the spices and transfer to the Air Fryer basket.
3. Bake at 360 degrees F for 8 minutes or until lightly golden. Work in batches. Bon appétit!

Zoodles with Cheese

Servings: 4
Cooking Time: 30 Mins.

Ingredients:

- 12 ozs. zucchini noodles
- 2 garlic cloves, minced
- 1/3 cup butter
- 2 tbsps. milk
- 1/2 tsp. curry powder
- 1/2 tsp. mustard powder
- 1/2 tsp. celery seeds
- Sea salt and white pepper, to taste
- 1 cup cheddar cheese, grated
- 1 heaping tbsp. Italian parsley, roughly chopped

Directions:

1. Place zucchini noodles in a colander and salt generously. Let them sit for 15 minutes to remove any excess water.
2. Cook in the preheated Air Fryer at 425 degrees F and fry for 20 minutes or until they have softened.
3. In a mixing dish, thoroughly combine the remaining ingredients.
4. Toss the cheese mixture with your zoodles and serve immediately. Bon appétit!

Herby Veggie Cornish Pasties

Servings: 4
Cooking Time: 30 Mins.

Ingredients:
- ¼ cup mushrooms, chopped
- ¾ cup cold coconut oil
- 1 ½ cups plain flour
- 1 medium carrot, chopped
- 1 medium potato, diced
- 1 onion, sliced
- 1 stick celery, chopped
- 1 tbsp. nutritional yeast
- 1 tbsp. olive oil
- 1 tsp. oregano
- a pinch of salt
- cold water for mixing the dough
- salt and pepper to taste

Directions:
1. Preheat the air fryer to 400oF.
2. Prepare the dough by mixing the flour, coconut oil, and salt in a bowl. Use a fork and press the flour to combine everything. Gradually add a drop of water to the dough until you achieve a stiff consistency of the dough. Cover the dough with a cling film and let it rest for 30 minutes inside the fridge.
3. Roll the dough out and cut into squares. Set aside.
4. Heat olive oil over medium heat and sauté the onions for 2 minutes. Add the celery, carrots and potatoes. Continue stirring for 3 to 5 minutes before adding the mushrooms and oregano.
5. Season with salt and pepper to taste. Add nutritional yeast last. Let it cool and set aside.
6. Drop a tbsp. of vegetable mixture on to the dough and seal the edges of the dough with water.
7. Place inside the air fryer basket and cook for 20 minutes or until the dough is crispy.

Tofu In Sweet & Spicy Sauce

Servings: 3
Cooking Time: 23 Mins.

Ingredients:
- For Tofu:
- 1 (14-ounces) block firm tofu, pressed and cubed
- ½ cup arrowroot flour
- ½ tsp. sesame oil
- For Sauce:
- 4 tbsps. low-sodium soy sauce
- 1½ tbsps. rice vinegar
- 1½ tbsps. chili sauce
- 1 tbsp. agave nectar
- 2 large garlic cloves, minced
- 1 tsp. fresh ginger, peeled and grated
- 2 scallions (green part), chopped

Directions:
1. In a bowl, mix together the tofu, arrowroot flour, and sesame oil.
2. Set the temperature of air fryer to 360 degrees F. Generously, grease an air fryer basket.
3. Arrange tofu pieces into the prepared air fryer basket in a single layer.
4. Air fry for about 20 minutes, shaking once halfway through.
5. Meanwhile, for the sauce: in a bowl, add all the ingredients except scallions and beat until well combined.
6. Remove from air fryer and transfer the tofu into a skillet with sauce over medium heat and cook for about 3 minutes, stirring occasionally.
7. Garnish with scallions and serve hot.

Fried Broccoli Recipe from India

Servings: 6
Cooking Time: 15 Mins.

Ingredients:
- ¼ tsp. turmeric powder
- ½ lbs. broccoli, cut into florets
- 1 tbsp. almond flour
- 1 tsp. garam masala
- 2 tbsps. coconut milk
- Salt and pepper to taste

Directions:
1. Preheat the air fryer for 5 minutes.
2. In a bowl, combine all ingredients until the broccoli florets are coated with the other ingredients.
3. Place in a fryer basket and cook for 15 minutes until crispy.

Crisped Tofu with Paprika

Servings: 4
Cooking Time: 15 Mins.

Ingredients:

- ¼ cup cornstarch
- 1 block extra firm tofu, pressed to remove excess water and cut into cubes
- 1 tbsp. smoked paprika
- salt and pepper to taste

Directions:

1. Line the air fryer basket with aluminum foil and brush with oil.
2. Preheat the air fryer to 370oF.
3. Mix all ingredients in a bowl. Toss to combine.
4. Place in the air fryer basket and cook for 12 minutes.

Veggies Stuffed Eggplants

Servings: 5
Cooking Time: 14 Mins.

Ingredients:
- 10 small eggplants, halved lengthwise
- 1 onion, chopped
- 1 tomato, chopped
- ¼ cup cottage cheese, chopped
- ½ green bell pepper, seeded and chopped
- 1 tbsp. fresh lime juice
- 1 tbsp. vegetable oil
- ½ tsp. garlic, chopped
- Salt and ground black pepper, as required
- 2 tbsps. tomato paste

Directions:
1. Preheat the Air fryer to 320 F and grease an Air fryer basket.
2. Cut a slice from one side of each eggplant lengthwise and scoop out the flesh in a bowl.
3. Drizzle the eggplants with lime juice and arrange in the Air fryer basket.
4. Cook for about 4 minutes and remove from the Air fryer.
5. Heat vegetable oil in a skillet over medium heat and add garlic and onion.
6. Sauté for about 2 minutes and stir in the eggplant flesh, tomato, salt, and black pepper.
7. Sauté for about 3 minutes and add cheese, bell pepper, tomato paste, and cilantro.
8. Cook for about 1 minute and stuff this mixture into the eggplants.
9. Close each eggplant with its cut part and set the Air fryer to 360 F.
10. Arrange in the Air fryer basket and cook for about 5 minutes.
11. Dish out in a serving plate and serve hot.

VEGETABLE & SIDE DISHES

Thyme & Garlic Sweet Potato Wedges

Servings: 2
Cooking Time: 30 Mins.

Ingredients:
- 1 tbsp olive oil
- ¼ tsp salt
- ½ tsp chili powder
- ½ tsp garlic powder
- ½ tsp smoked paprika
- ½ tsp dried thyme
- A pinch cayenne pepper

Directions:
1. In a bowl, mix olive oil, salt, chili and garlic powder, smoked paprika, thyme, and cayenne. Toss in the potato wedges. Arrange the wedges on the air fryer, and cook for 25 minutes at 380 F, flipping once.

Mint Fennel and Berry Mix

Servings: 4
Cooking Time: 12 Mins.

Ingredients:

- 2 fennel bulbs, trimmed and sliced
- 1 cup blueberries
- 2 ozs. mozzarella, shredded
- 2 tbsps. mint, chopped
- A pinch of salt and black pepper
- 2 tbsps. olive oil
- 1 and ½ tsps. mustard
- 1 tsp. coconut aminos
- 1 tsp. balsamic vinegar
- 2 tbsps. shallots, chopped

Directions:

1. Heat up a pan that fits the air fryer with the oil over medium heat, add the shallots, stir and cook for 2 minutes. Add the fennel and the blueberries, toss gently and take the pan off the heat. In a bowl, combine the mint with mustard, coconut aminos and vinegar and whisk well. Add this over the fennel mix, toss, put the pan in the air fryer and cook at 350 degrees F for 10 minutes. Divide between plates and serve with the mozzarella sprinkled on top.

Turmeric Cauliflower Rice

Servings: 4
Cooking Time: 20 Mins.

Ingredients:
- 1 big cauliflower, florets separated and riced
- 1 and ½ cups chicken stock
- 1 tbsp. olive oil
- Salt and black pepper to the taste
- ½ tsp. turmeric powder

Directions:
1. In a pan that fits the air fryer, combine the cauliflower with the oil and the rest of the ingredients, toss, introduce in the air fryer and cook at 360 degrees F for 20 minutes. Divide between plates and serve as a side dish.

Balsamic and Garlic Cabbage Mix

Servings: 4
Cooking Time: 15 Mins.

Ingredients:
- 4 garlic cloves, minced
- 1 tbsp. olive oil
- 6 cups red cabbage, shredded
- 1 tbsp. balsamic vinegar
- Salt and black pepper to the taste

Directions:
1. In a pan that fits the air fryer, combine all the ingredients, toss, introduce the pan in the air fryer and cook at 380 degrees F for 15 minutes. Divide between plates and serve as a side dish.

Simple Tomatoes and Bell Pepper Sauce Recipe

Servings: 4

Cooking Time: 25 Mins.

Ingredients:
- 2 red bell peppers; chopped
- 2 garlic cloves; minced
- 2 tbsp. olive oil
- 1 tbsp. balsamic vinegar
- 1 lb. cherry tomatoes; halved
- 1 tsp. rosemary; dried
- 3 bay leaves
- Salt and black pepper to the taste

Directions:
1. In a bowl mix tomatoes with garlic, salt, black pepper, rosemary, bay leaves, half of the oil and half of the vinegar, toss to coat, introduce in your air fryer and roast them at 320 °F, for 15 Mins.
2. Meanwhile; in your food processor, mix bell peppers with a pinch of sea salt, black pepper, the rest of the oil and the rest of the vinegar and blend very well.
3. Divide roasted tomatoes on plates, drizzle the bell peppers sauce over them and serve

Homemade Croquettes

Servings: 4
Cooking Time: 45 Mins.

Ingredients:
- 1 brown onion, chopped
- 2 garlic cloves, chopped
- 2 eggs, lightly beaten
- ½ cup grated Parmesan cheese
- Salt and pepper to taste
- ½ cup breadcrumbs
- 1 tsp dried mixed herbs

Directions:
1. Combine rice, onion, garlic, eggs, Parmesan, salt and pepper. Shape into 10 croquettes. Spread the crumbs onto a plate and coat each croquette in the crumbs. Spray each croquette with oil.
2. Arrange the croquettes in the air fryer and cook for 16 minutes at 380 F, turning once halfway through cooking. They should be golden and crispy. Serve with plum sauce.

Kabocha Fries

Servings: 2
Cooking Time: 11 Mins.

Ingredients:
- 6 oz Kabocha squash, peeled
- ½ tsp. olive oil
- ½ tsp. salt

Directions:
1. Cut the Kabocha squash into the shape of the French fries and sprinkle with olive oil. Preheat the air fryer to 390F. Put the Kabocha squash fries in the air fryer basket and cook them for 5 minutes. Then shake them well and cook for 6 minutes more. Sprinkle the cooked Kabocha fries with salt and mix up well.

Cilantro Broccoli Mix

Servings: 4
Cooking Time: 15 Mins.

Ingredients:
- 1 broccoli head, florets separated
- 2 cups cherry tomatoes, quartered
- A pinch of salt and black pepper
- 1 tbsp. cilantro, chopped
- Juice of 1 lime
- A drizzle of olive oil

Directions:
1. In a pan that fits the air fryer, combine the broccoli with tomatoes and the rest of the ingredients except the cilantro, toss, put the pan in the air fryer and cook at 380 degrees F for 15 minutes. Divide between plates and serve with cilantro sprinkled on top.

Cauliflower Falafel

Servings: 4
Cooking Time: 12 Mins.

Ingredients:

- 1 cup cauliflower, shredded
- 1 tsp. almond flour
- ½ tsp. ground cumin
- ¼ tsp. ground coriander
- ½ tsp. garlic powder
- ½ tsp. salt
- ¼ tsp. cayenne pepper
- 1 egg, beaten
- 1 tsp. tahini paste
- 2 tbsps. flax meal
- ½ tsp. sesame oil

Directions:

1. In the mixing bowl mix up shredded cauliflower, almond flour, ground cumin, coriander, garlic powder, salt, and cayenne pepper. Add egg and flax meal and stir the mixture until homogenous with the help of the spoon. After this, make the medium size balls (falafel) and press them gently. Preheat the air fryer to 375F. Put the falafel in the air fryer and sprinkle with sesame oil. Cook the falafel for 6 minutes from each side. Sprinkle the cooked falafel with tahini paste.

Cumin Brussels Sprouts

Servings: 4
Cooking Time: 15 Mins.

Ingredients:

- 1 lb. Brussels sprouts, trimmed and shredded
- ½ cup olive oil
- Juice of 1 lemon
- Zest of 1 lemon, grated
- A pinch of salt and black pepper
- ¼ cup almonds, toasted and chopped
- ½ tsp. cumin, crushed
- 1 tsp. chili paste

Directions:

1. In a pan that fits the air fryer, combine the Brussels sprouts with all the other ingredients, toss, put the pan in the fryer and cook at 390 degrees F for 15 minutes. Divide between plates and serve as a side dish.

Turkey Garlic Potatoes

Servings: 2
Cooking Time: 45 Mins.

Ingredients:
- 3 unsmoked turkey strips
- 6 small potatoes
- 1 tsp. garlic, minced
- 2 tsp. olive oil
- Salt to taste
- Pepper to taste

Directions:
1. Peel the potatoes and cube them finely.
2. Coat in 1 tsp. of oil and cook in the Air Fryer for 10 minutes at 350°F.
3. In a separate bowl, slice the turkey finely and combine with the garlic, oil, salt and pepper. Pour the potatoes into the bowl and mix well.
4. Lay the mixture on some silver aluminum foil, transfer to the fryer and cook for about 10 minutes.
5. Serve with raita.